Veggies 2

Veggies 2

Nature, Life, & Intimate Reflections

A Collection of Poetry

by

Marie Slow

ISBN-13: 978-0692393697
ISBN-10: 0692393692

Published by Marie Neumann on Createspace

Dedication

To all who made it happen

Marie Slow

Poems

A Brain

I reveal what is stored in my brain,
a wonderful storage, full of nooks,
memories and connections.
I can see my mother and brother clearly
I can not depict a picture of my father,
because I do not remember him.
I can reveal a thousand words at once
in both languages and the third chimes.
I cherish my brain and try to describe pictures,
memories when they are still there,
before an old age will cover them with mold.
The brain stores everything picked up
by my five senses and sometimes I think
it makes its own creations and combinations.
I smell fresh air after the storm
and see lightening crossing the sky,
the nature's wonderful fireworks
celebrating life. I smell lilac and jasmine
like it was yesterday when I was passing by,
freshly baked bread I could almost eat it.
My feet still remember about running barefoot
in the grass and through muddy puddles
and feel gentle mouths of tiny fish
nibbling my toes in clear water.

I hear a waterfall in the forest,
smell fern and spawn of mushrooms
after the rain. I feel a hand of my mother
and siblings, that wonderful sense of belonging.
I hear a laughter of my children
jumping into the water. I see
silent eyes of my daughter, who never told
what she was thinking, or I do not depict how
strong personality I was, before it is too late.
I still feel the pain when they were coming
to join us in this World a wonderful gift
of motherhood and feel very lucky
to live through all of this. I am walking
crooked bricks of a sidewalk and still hear
a man's voice watching me to smoke a cigarette:
I like them as much as you do, when I am
at my last cigarette. I hear all wonderful
songs. I see a child clutching
it's one toy under her arm and others
clicking their thumbs away sending
text messages to the friends just blocks away,
and not noticing a rainbow by the lake.
The World is divided since early childhood.
It is my wonderful brain, a gigantic storage
full of my memories filled by my five senses.

A Cave

I don't want to live in a cave.
It is inhabited by snakes.
I shall smoke there
and they will be hissing at me.
They even might bite
and in the night to crawl
into my warm leafy bed.

I don't want to live in the cave.
It is cold in winter.
There live insect eating bats,
they'll drop their food crumbs on me.

I don't want to live in the cave.
It is inhabited by the creatures.
Boars and feral swine
will come for a visit
when I shall be not around
to eat my food, drink my water
and sleep in my bed
and I shall not have
any private life.

I don't want to live in the cave.
There is outdoor plumbing
and cold water in the pond.
Heat is provided by a brown bear.
There are plenty berries,
but in winter they are scarce,
and no health care.
There are not taxes
on cave dwelling yet,
but Census already sent
its adversaries.

I don't know how to live in the cave.
I prefer warm home
and cool air-conditioner
with indoor plumbing.

Marie Slow

A Carrot

growing in soil
deep and deeper,
deep and deep.
"I show that beet
I can be as big as she!"
Besides   I   have
prettier color.
You hear about carrot hair.
Did you ever hear
about beet hair?
You are good for blood,
I cure eyes.
You color eggs red
and I can turn
skin yellow.
You are sweet
so I am.
They turn you into sugar
but rabbits like me more.

A *Cigar*

I am not going to put
my toe nail clippings
into your cigar,
while you are smoking.
I was joking.
I shall roll tobacco leaves
on my tights
to make one fat cigar
full of mouse droppings
and watch you inhale
with great satisfaction:
this cigar tastes great.
It is because your
twenty five wives
were rolling them
on their naked tights
and one was standing above
adding handfuls of droppings.

A Knot

We were told
it's time
to tie a knot.
How are we going
to do it?
He ties a reef knot
and I'm into
granny knots
granny knots.
He thinks
it's impossible
to untie
granny's knots .
It is not.
It is easy to tie
the reef knot.
I didn't even
make an attempt

to learn
to tie his knot.
How are we going
to tie the knot?
His knot, or my knot?
He can tie his knot
and I am tying my knot.
It's a time to tie
the knot
everyone says.
He has cold feet.
Next day my feet are cold.
Are your feet warm?
No.
We have cold feet.
Are we going to tie
the knot, or not?

A Gift

It is a gift.
They were taking.
Each of them
wanted to be
blessed.
They didn't
understand.
It is not
a blessing.
It is a curse.
Little voice
is whispering
a lullaby.
It is not you.
It is them.

A Life

Hold me in your arms,
hold me tight,
because today
I am going to die.
Tonight I don't see
stars shine, because tonight
I am going to die.
I shall wake up
tomorrow morning
to watch the Sun rise,
believing, believing
in goodness in people
and trust to no one.

A Maze

Two gray mice
lost in the maze.
One says,
come this way,
second oppose it,
no, we have
to go that way.
They get out of the
maze, run around,
so they could find
an entrance.
Running back
into the maze,
two lost mice
follow other mice,
and this is
how they found
their house.
We never go
there again,
said both mice.
It was one scare.

A *Spider*

A spider sitting in his corner
knitting destiny, jobs.
Sweater too short, mittens too wide
and scarves too tight.
Spider, why are you not going out
to sit and laugh
with other spiders alike?
To sit in the clubs,
or play golf
and talk stuff?
Why do you have to sit with us
to show us,
how you sit high above
in the corner
right under the ceiling light?
Nice view too.

Accident

He crossed the street on red light.
Nobody wanted to run over him.
The cars were colliding
and piling up,
horns were honking
and metal was hitting a metal.
Those on the back asked:
What happened, what happened?
Absent-minded pedestrian disappeared.
He threw away his jacket,
so nobody would recognize him.
He was probably ashamed
for what he has done.

Achy Family

I have a heartache,
you have a stomach ache,
she has achy feet,
a baby has an earache,
we have a toothache,
your hands ache,
they have a headache.
We are one achy family.

Marie Slow

After the door shuts

After the door shuts
and the footsteps die
she smiles,
pulls out
a sandwich and a bottle of coke
from a trunk
and begins to eat.

After the door shuts
and the footsteps die
she stretches
comfortably in the chair
and puts her feet
on the top of the trunk.
She eats and rests.
It was one busy day.

After the door shuts
and the footsteps die
she finished her supper,
reaches into the trunk
and takes out
a big faded notebook -
- a woman's diary.
She begins to read.

Air

Morning dew on the meadow
and in the mist I hear
a braying of the donkeys.
Salty air on the rocky beach
of the ocean
coming with the windy spray.
The beach is empty.
Only in the distance
is moving a lonely runner
away from me,
getting smaller and smaller.
Even a solitary dot disappears
in the grey morning
on the beach. Walking in the wind
to the nearest village.
My windbreaker is making
flapping noise
and a barking dog
barks in Morse code
how the wind
carries the sound.

I am catching
a breath in intervals
and try to walk backwards,
so I could gulp fresh air.
I am lying in the bed
watching my belly rising
rhythmically up and down.
I will be breathing
in and out
to the end of my days

Apes

I am getting a spot
in the zoo.
What do you
want me to do?
I am getting
an apartment
in primates
complex.
I shall be together
with all good looking
hairy apes.
Do not raise your hope,
the biggest and hairiest ape
looked me down:
no vacancy
in this homestead.
Find your dwelling
with molluscs
in underwater cave.

Bankrupt idealist

In the humongous
computer memory
are millions of slots categorized
by peoples' characteristics.
I am sticking out
from Bankrupt idealists box.
Do I like it?
Not.
But how I look around
at other boxes
in the department
of Human Psychology,
Territory: America,
in comparison with other slots
I settle down.
I still think I am well off.

Bark

Bark on the tree
Smooth grey
surface with dark
stripes
like zebra.
Grey, green and yellow
with many deep wrinkles
of an old man.
There is a stump
unevenly cut
when they took
a young tree down.
Why?

Naked branches
are reaching
to the wintry sky.
Trees are sleeping,
saving a sap inside
for the Spring to come.
Canadian geese
are feasting
on the green grass.

Beans' Goddess

She is walking down the mountain dressed in dry beans necklaces from her neck to the toes. The beans gently rattle. As she walks she tosses one necklace after another over dry fertile soil. Necklace of kidney, green, black, navy, pinto and wax beans she drops in Americas. She leaves lima beans necklace in Peru. Soy beans, azuka, and mung beans she throws over Asia and the necklace of fava beans is dropped in Europe. In her heels comes rain and thunder. When she is undressed she disappears in the river. She leaves flatulence as a little joke.

Marie Slow

Beautiful radishes

Beautiful radishes
on my table
tied in bunch
by rubber band
with green leaves
I cannot eat.
I gave them once
to a waiting horse
and he began
to pull his wagon,
I ran away.

Beautiful fresh,
red radishes
with such little
mice tails
of roots,
which feed
large red bulbs.

I can cut them,
make them to look
like roses
to decorate a plate.
I like to eat them
with bread and butter,
and perhaps,
a sliver of cheese.

Broccoli

Mr. Clinton likes broccoli.
Broccoli is hanging
limply on my fork.
I don't suppose to use
dressing or cheese topping
to make it tasty.
Crunch, crunch, crunch,
broccoli is getting
between my teeth.
Eat your broccoli.
I prefer cherry tomato.
Eat your broccoli.
Can I have veggie stromboli?
If broccoli is present
I shall not see it
It will be hiding
in the dough.

Brussels Sprouts

miniature cabbages
on the stalk

Bubbles

Bubbles got drunk
on sweet red currant wine
They float in the air
Bumping into clouds
Hiccup, hiccup, hiccup
It's not fair

Chicken day

For lunch we had a chicken.
For supper we are having a chicken.
Chicken nuggets
and chicken legs,
chicken thighs
are dancing
two step dance,
rumba,
and in the circle.
Chicken, chicken,
chicken here
and everywhere.
We are having
chicken day.

Cabbage

Its leaves tightly and neatly
packed into one big ball.
I do not say green leaves,
I do not want to discriminate
red cabbage which goes nicely
with a duck.
I didn't see anybody to eat
raw cabbage,
always prepared like
Chinese salad with garlic
and mushrooms,
stuffed pigeons stubbornly
called halupki,
Czech dumplings with cabbage
and pork
sprinkled with little bit
of caraway seed.
Leave my cabbage alone
means something like
mind your own business.

Today I had grilled chicken
with coleslaw
and a bun for lunch.
A jar with kimchi
broke in my suitcase once
so I had kimchi clothes
with kimchi shampoo
pajamas and shoes.
At block parties
I enjoy halushki with cabbage
and I ate thick Russian borscht
more than once.
I make cabbage soup
and a soup with kraut.
It looks like
everybody has use
for cabbage
made several ways
and it always tastes great.
You still don't care
for cabbage?

Clean Cat

Did you see
a cat eating grass?
"It will rain."
It has fur balls
in its stomach,
if you ask.
Yesterday
he pruned himself
white and orange
clean.
"We are expecting company."
We didn't get any, only the cat
with a tummy ache and his puke
all over the place.

Clean Cat 2

The cat is washing
his face.
Are we expecting
a guest?
He wants to be
clean
since his fur
doesn't repel
the dirt.
He has to do it
by himself.

Copyright

I am a philanthropist
giving away
my stories and poems
freely to humankind.
Take them.
They are on Internet
with no charge.
There is no money for medications.
Somebody pays my bills
and we can not
afford to go
on vacation.
Take them,
take them.
There is not
such thing
as copyright.

Corn

Maze
Green Sea
Sweet, dent corn, popcorn
Tortillas, tomatoes, porridge, cornflakes
Feed, poultry, livestock
Corn syrup, oil
Atole

Cucumber

For Q
Q- Q- Q- cucumber
cool as cucumber
and room temperature, too
cucumber   sandwiches
cues for salad
cues as shell
for another salad.
The ends
on the forehead
have cooling effect
cucumbers on the eyelids
are seeking youth

Q- Q- Q- cucumbers
and their multipurpose use
Cucumbers made into pickles
are smiling in the jars
on supermarkets shelves
next to mustard, ketchup
hot dogs and buns
ready to celebrate
4th of July.

Dead end

Stop sign
Halt
A man with
a red flag
Detour
Railroad crossing
The gates are down
Nobody have seen
train coming
for past twenty years
Another
stop sign
Red light
Another
red light
Missing bridge
Dead end
Dead end
Dead end.

Dancing flowers

Dancing flowers, dancing bees
and no dancing trees,
dancing ladybugs and scarecrows,
dancing Santa and snowman,
whole dancing garden
in winter on a window sill,
dancing penguins and dancing dancers
and nothing left for Christmas.
All of them are sold out
for this year.

Dancing sparrows and dancing blue jays,
dancing pigeons and dancing days,
dancing cars and chimneys
might be in the store next year.

Dancing shoes, left and right shoe,
stopped in the dark,
because they dance only in the Sun.
Dancing girl asks a flower:
"Will you dance with me?"
"No, thank you,
I dance only with a bee."
All dancing flowers are sold out
and I have nothing to give
under the Christmas tree;
only traditional stuffed bears,
jewelry, Barbie dolls
and other toys

Deer skin

Indians are walking
in rain.
It's a long trip.
They are dressed
in deer skin
and wearing
moccasins.
It rains and rains.

We put wet chamois
into plastic bag.
After some time
we began to sniff:
What is it?
Dirty feet? Dirty socks?
or a sewer pipe broke?

What Indians do
with their deer skins,
when they go to sleep?
Our chamois
is still out
in the rain
'till next wash day,
and before
I'll wash it
with soap and suds
and clean water
and then let it dry.

If you want
to use it,
put it under
running water
and it will soften.

Dentures

Plenty to eat
and no teeth.
They share one pair
between two of them.
I can't eat
with only upper part
and lower dentures
without top
just do not stick.
Lend me whole pair,
while I eat
and you can have
them back then.
I'll wash them,
I promise.

Why you don't buy
your own?
Yes, I share,
but I don't like
to share everything.
It seems to be icky,
yukky, ekelhaft.
Ron sells them
for fifty bucks.
He nicked them,
when their owner
took a nap.
Will they fit?

Diapers

Three years old boy
is learning
to do not wear
diapers.
Tony, let's change
your diaper.
Running away,
laughing.
His grandfather
is learning to wear
diapers.
It's a hard choice
to find such,
which will not leak
and take a big load.
Grandpa,
I don't want
your diapers.
They are too big
and they leak.

Domestic cat

Domestic cat
stands by the door,
patiently,
urgently,
demandingly,
because he wants
to go out.

He just discovered
outdoor life.
A jungle in the bushes,
and smells
of the garden.

He learns how to hunt,
or just to watch,
eat grass,
roll in the dust,
enjoying Sun,
wind and scents,
green leaves,
and wild life
in the garden.

Dream 1

Tell me
what are you
dreaming about,
when you sleep?
Your eyelids
and a tail
are twitching,
clenching your paws,
stretching your claws,
moving whiskers.
Tell me,
what are you
dreaming about?
You don't see
and you don't hear.

Dreams
(In Memory of MLK)

It is nice to have dreams.
Sometimes they reflect
daily worries.
I prefer to live
than die
for my dreams.
Dreams are just dreams.
I have to get up
in the morning
and watch sunrise
painting whole horizon
with its pastel fingers
dipped in pink, yellow,
purple and blue.
Hills are still asleep.
I am awake now
and I don't want
to die for my dreams.

Dreaming boy

A boy is looking into a window
well lit toy department store.
What he sees? Trains, cars,
video games, guitars and electronics.
He would like to have them all.
How he could play!
Hunger takes hold of him.
What is he going to do?
Take a rock, break a window
and take it all?
He approaches his mother
and they together walk
to the store.
He asks a store manager:
May I also have a toy?"
"Go away boy. Scoot."
He and his mother
walk together to soup kitchen.
Then they walk home.

He is dreaming:
One day, I shall grow up,
I shall have so much money,
so I could buy a whole store.
I shall have my own toy factory.
He takes a knife and a piece
of wood and carves a horse,
he will make in his factory.
He will get another piece of wood,
and he will carve whole farm,
with all farm animals,
and he will add an elephant,
and a tiger and a rhinoceros,
who will take mud bath
with farm pigs.
It will be unusual farm,
farm of his dreams.

Driving

You want me to give up driving,
because my driving is so bad.
We can save
little money
for gas, car insurance
and sell my car.
I'll be taking a bus.
The world around
will
drastically
slow
down.

Dunkin'

There is Dunkin'
Drive in
right behind
the comer.
Have a one or two
and coffee to go.
Come in,
have a coffee
over a gossip
with a twist.

Dying

I am lucky
I don't have to come
to visit my dying aunt
to say a tearful good bye.
All of them are already dead.
I am cynical.
My mother-in-law
was dying regularly
before Christmas
for about thirty years
and her son had to go
to say good-bye.
I didn't come along,
somebody had to take care
of two children, one cat
and tend the house.

My ex-mother-in law
is still alive.
I hope, she will be around
to one hundred and twenty five.
I know, I am cynical.
In the case
the aunt will not die
I shall apologize
and wish her
another healthy
and prosperous twenty five.

Eavesdropping

We can not
get rid of eavesdropping
TV channel.
We have about one hundred sixty
channels.
We go through all of them
on regular basis.
None of them say: I eavesdrop.
Some are silent,
some have nothing to offer.
Which one eavesdrops?
What we discuss
in our living room,
we hear on TV
and read in newspaper.
I guess,
we are not so unique.

English

His English is British
and bookish.
Wait for his sentence
to come up.
It requires daily practice
until he will sleep
and dream in English.
English opens
a door for him
to English speaking world
and the doorways
will be open always.

Extracting memories

Yes, you can.
No, you can't.
Sheltered childhood.
Different time zone.
Past time,
present time,
and the future.
Different culture.
When you dig
deep and deeper,
don't you envy
at least a little bit?
Even if you
will not admit?
Catholic background
for over one thousand
years.
All old traditions.
Don't you want
to become one?
Don't you envy?

Where is your past?
Yon have nothing
to hang on.
Views of artists
are different
from views
of greedy pigs.
What else?
Women's views
are different from men's.
Can you feel
like a woman?
No, you can't.
You throw a dirt
and look for dirt
in the people.
One day
you will die,
so I am,
and then we shall
… never meet

Fall

The wind
sweeps the leaves
down the street
and piles them up
in the corners.
Yellow, gold
for Fall,
red for season,
and brown for Autumn.
Trees are dropping
leaves
on the street
floor.
The trees
are shedding leaves,
before they go to sleep
in winter.

Flat headed cat
(To Natalie)

I have a cat
with completely
flat head.
We have a cat
with completely flat head.
You have a cat
with completely flat head
so ideal
to take it gently
into a palm
of one hand
and push it away.
The cat bites.

Fifth season

Now I have four legs,
so I can scratch my back.
What I need
is a tail
and one big mouth
to bark.
We are here
and we write.
We can also scream.
We are good
and getting better
with every year.
Oh, I forgot,
we write for fun.
We like to meet
and don't compete.
A bunch
of forgotten writers
from small town.
Don't give up!

It takes a time
to build up
a portfolio
and reputation,
which might sell.
Then we might change
and forget about
having fun.
What happened
to my tail?
Well, it has
to grow up, too.
Give it
another year
and it will add.
Meanwhile you can think
what kind tail
you would like
to have.
They will dock it,
was already said (and ears as well)

Flies and guillotine

Catch a fly,
carry it
to homemade guillotine
and execute it
French Revolution style.
"Mom, mom, look
what she is doing!"
It's only flies.
We kill them
all the time.
What's difference
between flypaper, fly swatter,
or guillotine style?
"How you would feel,
if somebody will
do this to you?"

"I am a child,
not a fly."
"She is a murderess
without feelings."
Stop killing flies
and clean up
the mess you made.
The windowsill is full
of beheaded, dead flies.
Little murderess
is sitting at the table
doing her math homework
with her tongue
sticking out

Flowers and colors

Seven kinds of flowers
in seven colors.
Colors mixed with green.
Springy wreath
is hanging on the door.
Spring is here.
Eggs in seven colors
lying in green grass
among white daises
and daffodils.
Children,
come with your baskets
and collect Easter eggs.
Don't step on daffodils.
Daisies will survive
the light steps
of birds and children.

Seven colors of seven
different flowers
in the vase
on the dining table.
Dinner is on the table.
Sit down,
it's time to eat.
Spring is here
chirp sparrows,
when taking
 their dust bath
creating holes
for planting flowers
 in seven colors
for seven children
living in grey house
down the street.

Footsteps

Following you
in your footsteps
looking for you.
Always too late.
Silent phone
conversations.
There is nothing
to say.
I am waiting,
but do not expect
you to come.
You are grown up.
I am here for you
unable to help.
I am fine. I am fine.
Do I hear
bitterness in your voice?
I'm supposed to be here,
and I was not.
"I am fine."

Fruit

Apples, oranges,
pears and plums,
all together
on the stand.
Strawberries, blackberries,
blueberries and other berries
made into jam.
Others are called preserves.
Kiwis, pomegranates,
bananas and pineapples
as exotic fruit
traveled far
to visit our land.
Not only grapes
are made into wine.
Wine can be made
even from dandelions.
Fruit is on the top
of food pyramid
and we can live
only on fruit as well.
I would not like to do
without meat.

Marie Slow

Forget-me-nots

Wind blew seeds
 of little blue flowers
into our backyard.
They are beginning
to bloom now
to remember.
Forgive-me-not,
forgive-not-to myself.
Do not forget
broken promises,
promises of mornings
forgotten by the evening
of the same day.
It wasn't I didn't
remember.

I was: who cares?
I didn't, others did.
By the end
I didn't have friends.
Forget-me-nots shyly
open their blue eyes
 to say: I am sorry
for what I have done.
Only to open old wounds?
Quietly tip-toe around,
or do not show up
and let time
to go by.

Fundraisers

To tell the worst about myself
and nothing good,
because you're not supposed to brag
about your good deeds.
What are my good deeds anyway?
Waking up in the morning
with a sign of a permanent guilt,
which doesn't leave too much room
for happiness.
Learning to be happy, at least three,
or four fund raiser letters
come to the mailbox every day.
Give, give, give!
I have milk to buy!
To be good, to be good
and nothing is left
for to live normal life,
even if it is so much fun.

Gardening

Carrots taste bitter.
Birds do not want
to nibble on our sunflowers.
In the moment
when they gather
on the garage roof,
there is a sound
of the bird of prey
coming from the cemetery -
junkers - dive, hide,
or you will be eaten.
Every day I pull weeds.
Wild strawberries
do not taste
like strawberries
in the woods
of my childhood.
In our garden
I grow weeds.

Garlic

Each clove carefully wrapped
in its individual skin
like candies in the store,
or a precious jewel.
All cloves are so perfect,
they create one ball.

Eat garlic when influenza
or vampires are in town.
Second day my skin and breath
reek of garlic.
I know something is missing,
when I eat some dishes -
garlic, garlic isn't there.
It doesn't taste the same.

Ghost towns

They are taking space
where should be fields and pastures,
because people left.

There is nobody
to tend to the graves,
and nobody to turn cemeteries
back to the fields and pastures.

Good Shepherd

There are not
good shepherds anymore.
They count money
and the souls.
I have a good shelter.
They feed me well.
I can buy clothes.
What I am looking for
 is a good shepherd
to comfort me,
to nurture my soul.
I don't want to walk
alone.

Hair Dryer

Hot air is blowing
into my hair.
Brushing it softly
with a brush
in my right hand
and separating
strands.
Left hand is holding
a hair-dryer
circling
around a head.
Changing hot button
to the warm fan.
Warm air
is noisily
drying my hair.

Harvest

Evil is making rounds
gathering human souls.
Please, hide my soul,
hide well my little soul.

Haunted

Haunted memories
living past
Beating myself with
imaginary stick
What I would do different today
and what I have done
under circumstances
and lack of experience
due to age.
I try to be happy
and many times
I succeed.
Guilt for enjoying reading.
They call it bibliotherapy.
Today I call it laziness
and many times
waste of the time.

Haunted 1

Haunted dreams,
haunted sleepless nights.
Mistakes and deeds
under magnifying glass.
Something cracks
in the wall,
quick footsteps
in the alley.
Is it a face
in the glass door?
Wind just knocked
a chair outside,
or was it a giant's breath?
Knock, knock
on the outer wall.
It is a loose wire.
Something is coming
to the kitchen...
An orange cat
came for his
midnight snack.
Another sleepless night.

Here and Beyond

Here and beyond
dining with immortals,
searching
for history in stone.
Selling quackery
for a dime
to fools,
gullible,
trustworthy
yesterday;
today duped.

How do you punish a mentally challenged?

How do you punish
a mentally challenged?
With a dandelion to her palm ....
Do not feed her?
Take TV privileges?
Put her into a cage?
We don't do that.
Change prescription,
add more pills,
take off some pills,
change a diet,
no fat diet,
vegetable diet,
so they will grow weak
I talk to them every day.
Somehow it doesn't penetrate.
Full bowl of porridge
brings a smile on her face.
More porridge, please,
and I shall behave.

Human Hands

Men's hands
putting together engines,
taking them apart.
Tinkering men's hands.
Hungry, impatient,
discovering, uncovering,
gentle, conquering
hands.

Women's hands,
gentle,
feather like touches,
threading a needle,
caressing, cooking,
washing dishes,
firm in touches.

Human's hands
distinguish us from animals.
Working, playing,
loving and hurting,
making, touching,
humans arthritic hands.

Hush Baby

Hush baby,
daddy will get you
every wish.
Hush baby,
have a hearty appetite.
I promise your daddy
I shall not interfere.
Hush baby,
I will not say a word.
Hush baby,
you may have it all.

In Memory

Flying, trying to learn
how to fly
when you are already
in the air.
The choice between being
barbecued alive or fly
without the wings.
It was long, long way down.
Safety switch which should turn
reality into video game failed.

Identity and Integrity

Identity met integrity
in the slums of New York.
It was like
hitting a brick wall.
Show your identity,
produce your identity card
and hold it tight.
It has a different name.
I know, it's handy,
when we make purchases.
Where is your integrity?
Show me your bag.
Where is it?

Show me your identity card
with your picture on it,
so you can be identified,
and your fingerprints,
if you want to get
teaching job.
There is a talk about DNA.
Don't forbid children
for spitting at each other.
Good spit might be
your next identity mark.
What about integrity?
It's in your bag.
Take it home with you.

In the dead of night

Going to the bathroom
and back to bed.
Listening to the sounds.
The fridge is humming,
the dog yelps
in his sleep.
The faucet in the bathroom
is dripping: drip, drip, drip.
I didn't close it properly.
I have to get up
and do it right.
Back to bed,
nice, warm bed.
Before I know
I am asleep
without dreams.
It's seven o'clock
morning
Sleepy day rains.

In the middle of the night 2

In the middle of the night
I hear a mouse
digging, scraping, gnawing
a hole
trying to get into the house
to be warm in winter.
The mouse is scratching,
digging, thinking:
I am sure
there will be some crumbs
and plenty of food, too.
The cat is asleep.
It was assault
to all felines.
It should be:
The cat is sitting
on the other side of wall
waiting for the mouse to show

Intolerance

With the eyes closed
and headphones
on the ears,
it's called a tunnel vision.
Don't realize
 it can be
somebody's first time?
Trying to ruin it,
trying to ruin
somebody's first time
successfully.
Succeeded.
What for?
For goodness sake!
Why did you do it?
What for?
With the eyes limited vision,
do not hear,
what is said,
do not see
what is felt.

Shutting off,
shutting out.
Trying to be practical,
when to be practical
is in the way.
Be yourself.
Who am I?
I am an old fool.
Everything was said
and nothing was
absorbed well.
I didn't hear you
knocking on the door.
Senseless senses,
dull senses,
closed eyes against beauty
so freely offered.
No highs,
no lows,
just one crippled
life.

Invented

To celebrate
human kind
for its inventions.
Restless, poking,
hard thinking minds
 how to do
something better.
Always looking for new
unknown paths
to walk, to thread.
A big book of inventions
of humankind
was already written.
Entries are marked:
 invented, invented,
with the year,
or at least a century
behind.
The nations proclaim
it was us who came
with a paper.

We came with a papyrus
before.
What about clay tablets?
Who began to write
in symbols?
What about an alphabet?
Each nation
 has its own.
Of course, before writing
there was a language.
The words, the syllables
and letters
to name people, things,
the verbs for action
and others to describe,
 to specify.
All of them were invented.
What a wonderful world
of unquiet
human minds!

I've always dreamed about...

what is on the other side of the hill?
There was a valley followed by another hill,
and another and another ...
What is behind the curve of the dusty road?
Lying on my back on the green grass,
I was wandering where the birds are flying.
"Take me with you," I dreamed.
"You are too heavy, and besides,
you have no wings to fly."
When my siblings were searching for me,
blamed for my disappearances,
they threatened me with gypsies:
"One day they will steal you,
break your arms and legs
and make you beg for your living.
"I wasn't afraid of the gypsies.
They have enough of their own children,
they do not need somebody else's.
I was wandering all day long,
but with the sunset, I wish to go home.

Jealousy

One evening
she showed up
at my steps
dripping wet
with envy
and jealousy.
There is so little
I can do for you.
Is life not treating you right?
Did I get
a better piece?
"One day
I will burn down
your house."
She was drunk.
She didn't burn
my house.
She changed,
she said.
She left
my steps
clutching
to her chest
my yellow shirt.

Kikimora

Kikimora
inhabited our house.
She is misplacing
and hiding things.
Where is she taking them?
For show and tell
to other kikimoras
how she has done well.
We are dropping everything
we touch.
Kikimora is knocking
full plate
out of my hands
to the floor.
I do not see
chicken feet.
You are just
imagining things.
What about missing
keys and utensils?
You are old
and do not remember
anything.

Kohlrabi

Pulled young, fresh
from the patch
at the Spring time.
The top and skin go
to the rabbit.
I eat the rest
cut in pieces,
crispy, crunchy, tasty.
Rabbit is twitching
its nose:
I would like
to get more.

Line

I didn't want to work
in a prison
for people who crossed a line.
Where is the line?
Everybody is crossing
to get faster
to the other side
of the street,
to get piece of neighbors
property for free.
To get a better job,
to get a job,
jump a neighbor's wife.
Everybody is crossing.
Then - where is the line?

Lucky Cat

I am one lucky cat.
It's freezing outside
and I am inside
in the warm house
sleeping in the bed,
on the top of sofa
and on the cushy chairs.
What I like the most
is to stretch
by the hot radiator
with my paws under it.
I am getting older
and I am one lucky cat.
Only food could be better.

Little Princess

Little princess, dear,
fulfill your promise,
 have no fear.
Walk in the dark
to the closet,
open door,
do not scream.
There is nothing to fear.

Little princess, dear,
have no fear,
walk to the library
in the darkness.
Do you hear the books
are whispering?
One day you will
know them all.

Little princess, dear,
don't walk to the forest,
do you hear?
What could you meet,
you never know.
Bad people,
fairy tale characters,
we don't know
they didn't exist,
or did they?
It's better
do not know.

Masks

What I see in their eyes?
They don't give away emotions.
Don't show any feeling.
Only a mouth gives away
thoughts, constructive ideas,
fast way of thinking.
Wear a mask.
Provide tears
when whole nation is weeping.
You have to wear a mask
to survive.
Do not show,
what you are thinking,
not even to your friends.
They are not friends,
only acquaintances and cliques.
Do not cry,
or you will become a joke.
One day I wanted to see
my face under the mask -
my real face.
The mask won't come off.
It became my face.

"Men"

What I do not
like about "men":
each of them
is looking
for mummy
to feed them,
take care
of them,
but there
is no daddy
to cover
the bills.

Marie Slow

Memories of the Nation

Hundreds of burned
down villages
like Czech Lidice.
Genocide of
Jews
Ukrainians
Poles
and Lithuanians ...
Terrors of the War
told to small children,
so they will know,
to remember,
because this is a history
of the Nation.

The stench of burned
human bodies
and the skulls and bones
of the family.
Some lost their minds
over this.
Pass quietly
by the graves and crosses.
Leave quickly,
move out, relocate.
Do not remember,
forget,
because there are lying
memories of the Nation.

Mice
(To Madigan)

I went out
to catch
some mice.
Here is
what I brought:

One shrew with whole
family of little shrews,
so tiny,
they are not worth a bite.
Are we letting them
grow up?
Are you crazy?
They will eat
us alive.

Two gerbils,
three house mice,
four deer mice,
one rat,
five titmice
(they speak English and they fly.)
Let titmice to the yard.

They'll eat flies
and other bugs.

Six field mice,
seven white footed mice,
eight hamsters
(not for eating by the cats.)
They are designed
as house pets.

Finally I brought
ten white mice.
They are alive,
if you want to eat,
you have to kill them first.
What do you want me to do
with the rest?
Sell gerbils and hamsters
to the kids.
They will give them a home.
The rest in the cage
with water
and some grain,
so they will be fresh,
when we are hungry again.

Middle Ages

Dr. Faust lives
just behind the corner.
Cardinal Richelieu
outgrew his diapers
long time ago.
Tomorrow the disciples
will bring the banned books
to the bonfire.

Inquisition is watching movies
and cuts out the scenes
endangering the morals.
There are so many copies "to edit",
so many books to read!

Moo-la

A statue
of a rather small cow
stands
in the middle
of the city square.
In her life
she produced
a number one,
with many zeros
behind
gallons of milk.
What the cow!

Morons

Morons are having a hay day.
Young female morons
are coming with shopping carts
to take what they think
they will need.
Why not? It's free.
Moroness is forcing
her way to the door.
I can do it. I am strong.
I can have it. It's free.
She just watches them
jump over the fence,
dancing on the floor
and singing morons song.
(this is how they
call themselves).

Motherly Love

How you will win
your children?
You will serve them
your siblings ...
One with spinach,
another with roasted potatoes
and the third one
with corn and rice.
How you will serve
your siblings
to your children?
With love.
There is something wrong.
This is what
the family is for.

Mumps

Mumps in wooden keg
are sitting on the table.
It was hard to choose
from all colors.
I like them all.
Finally I picked
rusty one,
the color of Autumn.
Too old to learn
how to paint?
Too lazy to learn?
To concentrate,
to try another way
and something new.

I think I would choose
watercolor, or pastel,
or both?
With the tip
of my tongue
sticking out
(childhood habit)
with a medium brush
and little one
I am trying to depict
first colors of Autumn
and grotesque
shapes of gourds
lying around the pot.

My best friend

Sharing food
with a mouthful
I declare:
You are my best friend -
today.
Tomorrow triple A
is towing my car
and when I see
their truck coming
I call a driver:
You are truly
my best friend.
Did I lose a sense
of friendship?
Did I lose a meaning
of the friendship?
Am I my best friend?
I don't think so.

My best friends
are those
who stop me
from doing:
Things without thinking
Correct my reckless driving
Through the life
They do it quietly.
Sometimes with a little remark,
or a gesture.
Sometimes just
with a stop sign
I cannot pass
unnoticed
and I have to stop
and think:
Why?

Naughty Children

Where is our mother?
She took a goat to a pasture.
Children jump on their beds.
Children, get dressed.
Children are laughing.
It's a pillow war.
Feathers are soon
snowing everywhere.
Janie, you will get
a spanking.
Mother walks the goat home.
She brings food on the table
and leaves a messy house as is.
She goes to milk the goat,
leans her head
against goats' warm side.
She can hear children
in the house shriek
and one is crying.
The goat quietly ruminates
and the mother thinks the goat
whispers soothing words
into her ear.

She walks back into the house.
She carries warm milk
in the pail.
A brush she uses
for scrubbing a floor
flies into the pail
full of warm milk.
Here is milk for you, children.
She walks back to a shed,
takes the goat
and they walk together
back to the pasture.
She cuts grass
so the goat will have
something to eat
in wintertime.
She comes back home,
cleans a table,
washes the dishes
and cooks a meal
for next day.
It is a matter of a habit now.
In the morning

(continued)

she takes the goat
back to the pasture.
She returns back
late in the evening.
Darkness looks inside
through a broken window.
We are hungry.
There are potatoes
in the field,
go, dig them out
and cook them
for your meal.
She walks back
to the shed
to milk the goat.
The goat lovingly
whispers into her ear.

New York City

We are going
to New York City.
Give us a tour
if your time permits
and we shall be
in awe.
Give a tour to two
older folks
through a Big Apple
and we shall look
like a calf
on a new gate.

One lucky cat! Is he?

A little kitten left his house
and a big yard he shared
with his brothers and sisters
and went to live in an apartment,
where pets are not allowed.
Another apartment he shared
with a big dog,
who liked to sniff his behind.
He traveled a lot
under a seat in the car.
He also lived and got evicted
from another house
and for three days
he lived in the car.
For six weeks he lived
on the upper shelf in the closet.
What adventures of life!

Don't call cruelty
against animals yet.
He always had his food,
water and litter box,
also a basic healthcare,
not a blue cross and blue shield -
just to get by -
and for Medicare he doesn't qualify.

One lucky cat
has whole house now,
litter box on each floor,
beautiful view from a window
to watch a wild life,
like birds, squirrels, rabbits,
bees, flies and butterflies.
Even a family of chipmunks
moved in. No hunting permit!
One lucky cat, is he? -
until a day a dog moved next door.

One Wish
(To Tanner)

One wish,
two fish,
three dirty
dishes
swimming
in the pond.
One yellow willow dipping legs
in bubbly water running over
its knobbly toes.

One wish
just flew away
on the back
of a blue dragonfly.

Whose wish?
 man's, woman's,
or a child's?
What wish?

I don't know.
It was colorful
like a balloon
and didn't have dollar signs.

The wish,
the size of a balloon, well fed
by untamed
fantasy.

One Sick Man

You are one
very sick man.
You want them all
and replace new with the old.
What do you do with them?
Give them away
for favors,
for their fame.

You are one
very sick man.
It is you
you have to blame.
You started this
and now
do not know
how to stop.

You are one
very sick man.

Onions

Onions on the wagon
Onions to the store
Onions in gold brown skin
Onion rings
Chopped onions
Onions for the salads
Strong, pungent, biting,
spicy onions.
Sweet onions
for delicate stomach
Always out of onions
Go to the store
to get onions
for the cooking
Onions for the sauces
Onions, onions, onions
Not enough onions.

Ostriches

Near a bridge,
close to a river
where there is a sand bank,
a row of emus stands,
heads buried
in the sand.
Wind blows
their tail feathers.
Pine tree looks down,
 its crown
is shaking, shaking, shaking ...
Then emus pull out
their heads:
they walk to get money,
take money to the bank.
"See you tomorrow,"
they say.
Pine tree looks down,
its crown
is shaking, shaking, shaking ...

Outside cat

You are not going out.
You roll there in dirt
and bring home bugs
and other stuff.

You are not going out.
You come back
with dust
in your fur
and shiny eyes.

You are sitting by the door,
waiting for me
to open for you.
Alright, you may go.

Parsnip

What am I going to do
with a big parsley root?
I shall wash it well
and put it whole
into good, strong beef soup.

What am I going to do
with the big parsley root?
I shall cut it
into small pieces
and add it to vegetable soup.

What am I going to do
with a big parsley root?
Wash it, clean it, boil it,
pickle it with vinegar,
serve it with food.

Potatoes

On Monday
potatoes from Idaho
On Tuesday potato soup
On Wednesday red potatoes
boiled in their skin
and sprinkled with parsley
On Thursday yellow
Yukon potatoes with meat
On Friday white potatoes
served with fish
On Saturday chicken
and potato salad
On Sunday a cake.

Peppers (honest confession)

They are green peppers
full of "poison",
because they didn't
have time to ripen.
Red peppers had that chance.
They are called sweet peppers.
Then they are yellow peppers.
They're suppose to be democrats.

Long time ago somebody fed me
with peppers marinated in oil
to take the poison out
prepared by his mom.
They were a delight.

Peppers were OK.
as they say
until one night
I ate three day old
green peppers ("poison" ones)
already cut in stripes.
That night I was very sick.
You can have
all the peppers in the World,
you also can have mine.
I am done.

Potatoes 2

One, two, three
small potatoes,
four, five, six small potatoes.
Add one egg, salt,
some onions,
it is how to make
blennies.

Skip onion, add garlic
and marjoram.
It is a recipe
for potato pancakes.

Rotten potatoes,
shriveled
mother potato with
white shoot,
which would like
to grow
into new potato.

Pumpkins

Pumpkin field,
orange lanterns
dressed for Halloween
Pumpkin seeds
and pumpkin pie
The biggest pumpkin
and many small ones
ready for carving
of scary or funny faces.
Look, pumpkin field
is in town.

Points

Pointy pencil and nothing catches attention to draw.
Pointy bra made for reason to
always catch hungry men's eyes.
Pointy shoes just to change fashion and
squeeze toes together -
what a relief to take them off in the evening!
Don't forget you have PowerPoint presentation tomorrow!
Yes, I have got your point after our rather lengthy conversation.
A cow pointed her long horns at trespassing tourist.
Suddenly I miss my little quiet world
without a presence of my older brother,
who was just dumped by his date.
Tell him a single word would be pointless.

Winter fruit

A bush is covered
with sparrows
looking at me.
They are hungry fruit
of winter.

Questioning

I stand in front of him.
He is too tall,
I can't see his eyes
and I look into his chest.
Where are you from?
Former Czechoslovakia.
What is it now?
Czech Republic
and Slovalcia.
And which one
are you?
What happened?
They decided
they don't want to be
together anymore,
so they divorced.

Without a war?
Without the war.
Do you have any ...?
He meant grudges
only didn't want
to say it.
No, my sister-in-law
is Slovak.
They are more
temperamental,
that's all.
And maybe not,
I don't know.

Quiet Life

What does it look like
to have a simple life?
Wake up in the morning,
listen to the birds,
talking about weather
and how to dress.
Make coffee,
have breakfast
and read a paper.
What are you doing today?
The same as every day:
little dusting, little cleaning.
What are we having for dinner?
Learning to cook on higher level,
with more imagination.
Talking to the neighbors,
playing with the cat.
Then comes an evening.
What did you do all day?
The same as every day.
Where did it go?
I don't know.
There is no drama,
just little quiet life

River

River
magnificent
swelled with water
swift
home of ducks
mighty

Santa Claus
(for Joe)

Dear Santa,
this year is your turn
to sit
on somebody's lap
and tell him
your wishes.
You wish
for good health
(forget about bottle of whisky)
and many years
of good service.
You wish
for your grandchildren
to sit on your lap
all year around.

Merry Christmas, Santa.

Zucchinis

Long green zucchinis
are hanging down
from a canopy.
Shadowy green tunnel
leads to a green door.
Zucchinis are unlit
lanterns,
ripe season of harvest.
White chair on the deck.
I cannot sit down,
I am only passing by.

Sausages

I am on a pill
to lose an appetite
to crave sausages.
My stomach is upset,
because smoked sausages
would like to get.
Sausages and smoked meat
Hungarian salami,
smoked ham,
and honey cured ham,
spiraled ham,
hard salami,
turkey ham
with mustard,
horseradish or dijon.
Everything smoked
I want to eat.
I drool over sausages

on the stick,
or as a cold meat.
I eat a carrot,
lettuce and spinach,
red apples for lunch.
Then I go for walk
to watch
smoked rabbits
flying by
still in their
fur coats.
I have vivid dreams
about smoked sausages -
my heart delight -
sausages in their tutu
dancing one leg cancan -
and smell
is just irresistible.

Short lived loves

Who is going
to bless
short lived loves?
I want,
I want,
I want.
She has better piece of a pie.
He slept with
your wife.
He is what I want.
Dogs are enjoying
themselves without love.

Listening
to our urges,
to our drives,
to cats instincts
to multiply.
Where is love?
What is love?
Not to one man,
or a woman ...
Illusions,
long overdue bills,
wasted tickets,
discarded
one night stands.

Second day after President Lincoln's Birthday

Children in the class
are exchanging the cards
full of affection.
Some get a lot
and some just
the card from their homeroom teacher
who understands
how it feels
to not be popular.
Most favorite girl
gathers an overflowing box
and walks proudly home.
It is her day.

One winter day,
when a muscle
 in the chest
supposed to beat faster,
little winged, naked brats
are sitting outside on the bush
since early morning

armored with weapons
they borrowed
from huntress Diana.
Do not feed them,
better do not go
out whole day.
They don't aim well,
last year produce seller
 fell in love
on this day
with used car dealer's wife.
The dealer cut his tires
and the produce seller
threw rotten cauliflowers
all over his house and yard.
It took a while
to sort things out.

Savoy cabbage

It says in a dictionary.
I didn't notice it in produce.
Is it a cabbage with a perm?
It tastes different.
It goes well with a lamb.

Silent book

I opened a book
with white, silent,
empty pages.
Nothing to read.
Too much to write.
Afraid to write?
Nothing personal.
There were
just reflections.
I liked to write
and now
I am afraid.

Silly cat

what are you
going to do
with your tail?
Stick it
in my soup,
or twitch it,
because something
bothers you?

Soul mate

How can I have a soul mate
with all doors closed,
windows locked
and barricaded basement?
Only birds can
occasionally poop
through the roof.

How can I have a soul mate,
when I don't know
much about myself?
Hey, knock on my head
and introduce yourself:
I am your soul mate.
Soul mate, who?

Only in children's games
we were soul mates
before we separated
to serve our boyfriends.

My sister, my sister,
where are you?

Soul searching

whole night
in friendly tavern
we were drunk
on spirits.
It was red wine.
Beer isn't good
for soul searching;
it's rather dull.
What did we celebrate?
The end of exams
and arrival of scholarship.
At 4.00 o'clock in the morning,
what did we find?
"The life
is like a ladder
to the chicken coop: short
and full of chicken poop,"
declared a garbage man
sitting next to us,
before he left to make
Prague beautiful.

The tavern closed
and there was a
two hours walk
to our dorms.
It sobered us up.
The birds were
welcoming
new day
and four drunks
were discussing
bits and pieces
of philosophy
jumping from Bacon
to Avicena,
from Decartes to Aristotle -
and back.
I don't remember
what it was about.
I was drunk.

Soul mating

Soul mating
is going alright.

Only other body parts
are getting rusty.

Squeezing

Squeezing orange juice
out of oranges,
crushing tomatoes,
and making apple cider.
Squeezing lemons
into tea,
eating apple core,
feeding leftovers
to the pigs,
making them drunk
on grape skins.
Sun drying raisins
and apricots,
preserving fruit.
Squeezing juicy oranges,
drinking tomato juice,
and crushing pineapples.
Squeezing good
to the last drop,
disposing pulp.

Spooks

I walk down the street.
On the left side
there is a cemetery.
There are houses
On the right
Ready for Halloween
night.
Each of them decorated
With some kind
Of spook.
Bloody corpses
Sitting on the porches.
One of them
Is pinned to the wall.
Ghosts are everywhere.
White skeletons
With big toothy grins.
Hand-carved pumpkin heads
Sitting on the steps

Together with pots
Of autumn flowers.
Even the apartments have
Something scary
In the windows
Like flying witches
On their brooms
Or cooking in the cauldrons
Their homemade brew.
It is one spooky town
And it will be full of spooks
On trick-or-treat night,
When children
Will be collecting
Their sweet dues.
Dead
in the cemetery
across the street
are waiting
for All Saints Day.

Spooky 2

I collect pictures.
I also collect
old photographs.
I do not know why
they look
so abandoned
 in thrift stores
and antique shops.
They sell very cheap.
I have
somebody's parents
and extended family
hanging above
my fireplace.
Uncles and aunts
decorate entrance hall.
Whole collection
of babies
and little children
claimed
dining room walls.
Serious faces

even invaded
the basement
and attic.
I tried to look
for likeness
and match
families together,
but it's impossible.
Nobody smiles on old
black and white,
yellowish dark
 photographs.
I tried to make
 stories
about one aunt
dressed in frilly
dress with umbrella.
She gave me
a dirty look:
"Don't tell lies."
Now she hangs
in one dark comer
in the basement.

(continued)

Somebody asked me:
"Aren't you afraid
they will haunt you
in the night?"
No, they don't haunt.
They just stare
and look like
completely misplaced
collection
of old photographs
waiting
for their families
to be claimed,
cherished
and to be proud.

Yes, the aunt
was right.
I lied.
I do not collect
old photographs,
so do not come
to our house
to claim
your ancestors.
To me
all of them
look alike.

Strawberry man

There was a man
who enjoyed eating
strawberries every day.
Strawberries in cereal,
strawberry dumplings
for lunch,
and after tea he asked:
what is for dessert?
Strawberries with whipped cream.
He enjoyed strawberries
pineapple and ananas
and all kind of strawberries
all year round.
Homegrown strawberries in summer,
strawberries from California,
Florida, Mexico and Arkansas,
when there was
winter in Pennsylvania.
When there was too much rain
he said:
bring me strawberries
from Spain.

Stream

How to get
out of the pond
full of fishes
to a little stream
with fresh water?
Little fish
has to practice
leap,
leap and twist,
over the bank
to clear,
fresh water.
Then swim,
swim fast
as she can,
against current,
so it will not
take her back
to the pond.

She has to
keep trying
and practicing
whole summer.
Think about tactics
during the winter
as she grows
bigger and stronger.
At Spring time
she will swim
upon the stream
to eat all bugs
and dragon flies
and return back
to the pond
for winter time.

Sudetenland

An old cemetery
overgrown with rhododendrons
with iron fences and gates.
We are reading German names.
Sometimes we come
to read poetry,
because it is quiet here
and we feel
romantic or morbid?
We are teenagers,
we didn't know
these people - they are dead.
Their relatives are in Germany,
or dead.
We are new here,
our families came
to populate Sudetenland.
Maybe we are reaching
for connections,
curiosity about people
who came here
long time ago,
or we just like
overgrown rhododendrons.

Sunflowers

Sparrows are feasting
on sunflower seeds.
If you eat them now
in winter time
you will have
nothing to eat.
A cat is patrolling
in sunflower patch.
He is not there
all the time.
Sparrows don't understand.
They want to eat now.
The cat is taking a nap.
When he wakes up
he walks into the patch
full of empty sunflower
shells.

Thank you for a life

It seems my pity for people dried up.
At least for those who ask for it.
I rather look into eyes beaten up by life
are shuffling near the wall to do not offend anybody
and do not become a target for their foul play.
I am looking for their eyes. I cannot find them,
because they even avoid an eye contact
just in case, they do not wish to upset anybody.
They have human eyes. The eyes which do not expect
human kindness and friendly words.
They are clutching their little worn out purses
to their chest with their meager savings
to buy milk and bread.
Thank you, I can get by. They took my cereal
and pennies I was saving in a box.
They are asking for an apartment number
of those who live alone.

They are afraid to get out of their apartments,
their only save place to live, to remember.
I am the last left. All my family is gone.
What choice do I have
when I don't want to live in a cave?
Thank you for a roof above my head,
cold and hot water, thank you for a fridge
and a stove, and above all
flushing toilet and a shower.
Thank you for few friends I can talk to.
Thank you for free food given by friendly faces.
Thank you for free Sun, rain and night's darkness.
Thank you I slept well last night.
I am meeting shortly my daughter.
I am lucky to have her.
I am alive and others are dead.
Thank you for my life.

The first time

The first time on the train.
It was a long ride,
early spring time
and meadows full
of yellow primroses.
First time on the plane
and didn't have a seat
by the window.
Today I sleep,
so I don't care.
Let others have
their first time.
First time
in heavy traffic
bypassing Washington, D.C.

Dry mouth
and butterflies
in the stomach.
Perhaps,
you would like to hear
about the first date.
Spare me embarrassment.
They are still
many "First times".
Each day is a new day.
Every day I meet
somebody the first time -
and it is a small town.

The end of the World

They were told
the end of the World
is coming.
So they gathered
in the basement
and sat there.
They brought with them
food and water,
blankets, pillows,
flashlights and candles.
They sat
in the basement,
holding their hands,
 and waiting.
They are hugging each other,
sitting in the basement,
holding the hands,
praying - and waiting.

One day
they walked out.
The World is the same
as was before.

Fall

Leaves change colors
brown, rusty, golden, yellow
beautiful Autumn

Leaf

Leaf in the water
floating, quietly, motionlessly
sign of the Autumn

The River

The river travels to the sea.
It cannot flow up to the hill.
It runs downhill,
pushes through a ravine.
How does it know,
which way to go?
Where is the sea?
And which sea
is its destiny?
It pushes its waters
through the plains.
Each drop knows
where it goes
and nothing can hold it.

It runs around obstacles,
creates islets and islands,
bends, depressions,
glens, gullies and valleys.
It eats away trees,
creates canyons
and waterfalls.
Nothing can stop it
until it becomes
a part of the sea,
or the ocean.
The waves wash the sand
at my feet.
They whisper:
we used to be Hudson river once.

The Seaside

It was Spring 1969,
when I met the Ocean
first time
in my life.
We knew
it is somewhere
near.
We ran, stumbled,
walked over one dune,
crawled over the second ...
Didn't believe
we will really get
to see
The Ocean.
It will be only
dunes, and more dunes,
and no ocean.
There it was.
Vast, majestic,
endless, calm
waves with white caps
- and more sand

to walk closer.
We danced, jumped,
hopped and pranced,
 recited a poem
by Czech classic
Jan Neruda.
The poem we completely
didn't understand
in time, when we have to
memorize:
"The sea,
you don't care
about my grief."
It was the end of May
and ocean was
in England.
We rolled up
our pants
and ran
into water.
Water was icy cold.

(continued)

We backed off
and ran again
and again
into water.
Yes, it was salty.
On the bridge
nearby stood
a group of people
and observed
three crazy Czechs
who came to dip
into the Ocean
in the month of May.

The Steps

It's the steps.
My foot was
all night aching.
A flat is nice,
yes, I like it.
Can you fly?
Can you walk
on your knees
and slide down
on your behind?
I cannot run
the steps up and down.
Sorry, I can't take it.
It's the steps.

The Store

Opens a store
early in the morning.
Stands behind a counter
whole day long.
For forty years
sells aspirin,
cough medicine,
condoms,
feminine needs,
knows the store
like a palm
of her hand.
Sometimes arrives
something new.
Where are we going
to put it
for our customers?
Go back to school
supplies
are on the shelves.
She is married
to the store.
What about the store?
The store feels the same.

The Unicorn

I am curious
what are they
going to do
with the pictures
of the people
who passed away?
What are they
going to do
with the photographs
of deceased people?
I think, they want them
baptize and convert
to their church.
Nothing else occurs to me.
My good luck.
Otherwise I would sit,
from sheer terror,
on the hot stove.
 Faith is dying,
Faith is awakening again.
Yesterday the unicorn
was shot to death.
Thousands of people
lit their candles.
I pray with them.

Marie Slow

To Shannon

There is one sad,
empty chair.
When is she
corning back
and put on
her thinking cap?

Tomatoes (tongue twister)
For Hailey

Tom and Tammy pick tomatoes.
Tammy picks tomatoes in the tomato patch.
Tommy trots to the tomato patch,
trips over No trespass sign
and talks to Tammy:
"Tammy, give me a tomato."
"Why don't you take an empty basket
and help me to pick tomatoes
in this tomato patch?
Tomatoes are ripe and they have
to go tomorrow to the market."
Torn and Tammy pick tomatoes.
They are round, smooth, soft
and red like Tammy's cheeks.
Tommy takes tomatoes to town today.

Tomatoes 2

Planting Sierra, Boa and Buffalo tomatoes.
Growing cherry tomatoes, teaching to climb cherry
and toy boy in Florida.
Some like yellow tomatoes.
Training Tiny Tim, Red Robin and Small Fry.
Pruning Early Girl, Prairie Fire, Moskvitch,
Better and Valley Girl.
Protecting Better, Super and Big Boy
from bad weather, bugs and caterpillars.
Harvesting Big Girl, Pink Odoriko,
Dad's Mug, Big Beef and Pink Ponderosa.
Cooking Milano, Roma and Green Zebra
with pleasure.
Eating and savoring all tomatoes.

I used Heritean Jacqueline 'Ortho's complete guide to vegetables.' Des Moines, Ill., 1997. Pp. 129-137

Tomato 3

Holding in both hands
smooth, soft roundness.
Cut into slices
quietly savor each seed.
Do tomatoes ever get
wrinkles?
No, they get eaten,
or they rot.
To savor each
beef tomato,
crunch on cherry tomato
in the salad
and wait for juice
to explode into lettuce
inside of my mouth.
Slice of tomato, onion
and lettuce create
a perfect harmony
on the top
of hamburger
(no mayo, please).

Marie Slow

Traitor

First we fed the birds,
then we let out a cat.
Birds are now singing:
traitor, traitor, traitor.
In my ears is their singing
ringing: Traitor, traitor ...
The cat sleeps,
his full belly
rests on the pillow
and his whiskers
are twitching.
He dreams
about catching
another bird.
Today he was well fed.
Traitor, traitor, traitor ...

Today, the cat
will not go out.
Birds call him
ugly, nasty names,
and tell him,
what they are going
to do to his: liver, spleen, eyes,
and other body parts.

Tree stumps

What are they doing with tree stumps
when Christmas trees are gone?
Do they dig them out,
or do they move the Christmas tree farm?
What happens to the trees' stumps
after the Christmas tree farm is gone?
Old pioneers knew the answer
when they were clutching trees
to create a land for farming.
Old tree stumps are fighting back
trying to break
farmer's and horse's back.
Some have to stay in the ground.
They prefer to be petrified.

Truffles

I am a pig
I love truffles
French also
love truffles.
They tie a rope
around my neck
and take me
for a walk.
I like to go
for a walk.
I look for truffles
I smell truffles
I root up truffles.
They pull me away
from my treasure,
they dig out truffles,
they eat my truffles
and I get pigswill.
I love truffles.

Turbines
(Unofficial training for bats and other birds)

Wind turbines are here
and more will be coming.
They already killed your parents,
siblings
and other relatives.
Fly high, fly low.
You can bring your predators
right to them.
Just learn and learn quick.
You are smart birds and bats.
Fly high while you are
on long trips
and avoid airplanes.
You can hear them coming.
Take detours.
Turbines are here
for good and they stay.

Twilight Zone

Shattered dreams,
or no dreams.
Shattered lives.
Dysfunctional families.
I can if you can,
playing dare,
crying games,
what have I got
myself into?
People looking
for themselves,
because they do not know
who they are
and sometimes afraid
to look into
dark shadows
of their memories.
Looking for connections,
listening, discovering,
searching, divorcing,
marrying, dying.

Two cutthroats (Tongue twister)

One cutthroat says to another cutthroat: I'll cut your throat if you will not give me your food. If you will try to cut my throat I'll first cut yours and let your blood ooze. So these two cutthroats cut their throats, their heads are now loose, separated from their bodies, two cutthroats will not eat each other food.

Peas

Peas, green round peas,
you don't want me,
my little Joe,
you don't want me anymore.
I don't want you,
I don't love you,
I even don't like you,
because yesterday evening
you went to steal with me.
I took you to the field
and you went on your knees
and stuffed pea pods
under your shirt, your parka
and into all pockets.
I didn't see any other girl
so scared like you.
Peas, peas, green pea pods,
we were leaving skins behind
as we walked.
You are not going to tell
anyone,
or you will be not my friend
and I shall not take you
to steal with me anymore.

Two headed chicken

I am not asking
two headed chicken,
why it has two heads.
It was born that way.
I just feel uncomfortable.
Chicken, I do not wish
to be your friend.
Why you don't look
for other two headed
chickens on Internet?
My space, perhaps?
You could have
 lovely conversations
pecking each other
two heads
at the same time.
I don't want you to move
into my head
with your two heads
and one body.

Which head is in control
of your two feet?
One beak is pruning
your tail feathers,
while another one
wants to eat.
I cannot be your
friend.
Go on the Internet
instead.

Marie Slow

Watermelon

As a child
I liked to eat
slice of watermelon
sitting on the steps
with my siblings
and spitting
black seeds
on the sidewalk.

I wished to eat
watermelon
in swimsuit
in the bathtub,
red juice
from ear to ear
dripping down
my chin.

I still count
how many
watermelons
I can eat
each season.

I am civilized now,
 refrigerated slices
cut into
little cubes
and watermelons
have no seeds.

What is wrong with you?

What is wrong with you?
Are you bipolar, kleptomaniac,
or sexually dissatisfied?
Are you a gang leader,
night prowler,
or plainly a hat bowler?
What is wrong with you?

Winter day

A shadow of a bird
is hopping over a snow bank
looking for poppy seeds
falling off poppy seed kaiser bun.
A nice treat to eat.
The bird is pecking grayish blue seeds.

Will you stand by me?

Will you stand by me,
when black birds
are circling the skies
and I have nowhere to go?

Will you stand by me,
when I cannot sleep
and a night is too long?

Will you stand by me,
when I feel lonely
and the World
is too big for me?

Will you stand by me,
when I will be learning
to walk with my head up,
instead of facing the ground?

Will you stand by me,
when I will be learning
to smile and have fun,
because the days
of paranoia are over?

Will you stand by me,
when I am looking for friends,
finding friends,
stretching my hands
and meeting their eyes?

Will you stand by me,
when I will be falling down,
down to the darkness
of the night?

"What, the heck,
are you doing downstairs
in the middle of the night?"

Wooden Fingers

I cannot have
my old job back.
My wooden fingers
can't type anymore.
Stiff fingers like
their rest.
Somebody else does
all the typing.
Not me,
I don't want
my old job back.
Pain in the wrists.
I learned to type wrong.
There was no time
to improve my skills.
Or was it?
Fingers say no
and my eyes blink,
when they see
a computer screen.

I like to watch
the birds,
blooming flowers
and their petals
slowly open
to the Sun.
I like to see
bumblebees and bees.
Watching brown rabbits
eating blossoming clover leaves
one by one,
maybe five
and then hop
to the neighbors garden
for slightly different diet
of variety salads
for tonight supper.

I don't want to type
anymore. I am done.

About The Author

Marie Slow is the pen name of Marie Neumann.

I spent the first thirty three years of my life behind the iron curtain. In 1981 I followed my ex-husband to the United States. English is my second language (www.betabitches.blogspot.com). I also write in Czech www.aalfons.blogspot.com. I self published (with lot of help) in the Czech Republic a book called *Aber die Konzen* (But those ends) which I wrote in 1976.
I am a member of POW! (Pottsville Writers) and regularly contribute to GROW (England).